Maltese bus history summary

1905 First bus imported into Malta. Electric tram services commenced.

1922 First bus service, Sliema – Valetta, commenced.

1929 Tramway closed around this time.

1931 Malta Railway (Rabat – Valetta) closed. It had opened in February 1883. A Traffic Control Board established; each of the 11 routes (now properly timetabled) assigned a colour.

1955 Traffic Control Board redistributed buses into 21 routes for Malta and one for Gozo.

1971 Change of Government. Dom Mintoff elected Prime Minister; one of his election pledges was to reorganise Public Transport.

1973 Following a strike over pay, all buses put into three groups with their own management and colour. Previous route colour system abandoned. Old destination boxes replaced by numbers inserted in metal boxes front and nearside; later front and rear.

1977 Malta Bus Service Co. (nb: not a company owning the buses) formed by merging previous three groups. All buses now painted spray green.

1979 Government authorised buses to travel without a conductor.

1980 New system of registration numbers introduced, eg Y-0300-M. Previously numbers only used.

1981 50+ ex-London Transport vehicles arrive, followed by 15 Bristol LH and 7 Leyland Tiger Cubs.

1984-7 170 Bedfords and Fords with Duple or Plaxton bodies arrive. Subsequent purchases bring this figure to around 250.

1989 Public Transport Authority established by Act of Parliament.

1995 Colour changed to warm yellow with dark orange band. Present registration system introduced. ("Y" replaced with DBY, EBY and FBY). Current Public Transport Authority decided that new buses should be super low floor and five 45 seaters (1 Optare, 2 Dennis/East Lancs and 2 Dennis/Plaxton ordered). Approximately 150 owners pay Lm500 each deposit for new vehicle, entitling them to a subsidy when delivered.

1997 First five new low floor buses delivered from UK as above.

2001 First non-UK imports arrive; Chinese King Long and Chongqing.

2003 Significant numbers of new generation low floor buses begin to enter service. The specification had now been revised from the original one; eg : engines complying with Euro 3 emission levels now required.

Note: The Public Transport Association comprises approximately 400 bus owners and is responsible for the day to day operational management of the service. It has a small management committee of elected owners and is responsible for collecting all revenue and sharing this amongst the bus owners on a fortnightly basis.

Malta Bus Album

A pictorial record of buses in Malta & Gozo spanning fifty years

Venture publications

INTRODUCTION

The island of Malta, located at latitude 36ºN, enjoys a typically Mediterranean climate, with untold opportunities for sightseeing and holiday making, whilst also, for the bus enthusiast, offering an unrivalled glimpse into the past. Its chequered history, with influence from Arab and Turkish architects going back many hundreds of years, provides a wealth of variety for the visitor; forts, churches and many splendid public buildings are, almost without exception, magnificent, whilst the Grand Harbour at Valletta with its constant to-ing and fro-ing of boats large and small in amongst the huge cruise liners is a must for anyone with a spirit of adventure. At around three and a half hours flying time from the UK it is, in all truth, quite accessible – and most people speak good English!

As the economy is gradually being swung to a tourist-based one, some of the traditional charm is inevitably being lost. Nowhere is this more true than in the realms of public transport where, unfortunately in some ways, change is now occurring at an ever-increasing tempo. Whilst there are at the time of writing (December 2003), literally hundreds of pre-1970 buses operating on the island, the older gems are now being replaced with modern low-floor imported machines, mainly from Turkey or China, but also from Greece, Macedonia and Poland.

Part of the cause of this revolution is the island's legislators' determination to curtail the number of journeys made by car, thus reducing pollution and congestion. More attractive, easy-access buses, they argue, will help. Now is therefore the time to make the pilgrimage, whilst old and new are operating side by side, and in so doing to turn back the clock and see what bus operation in the UK was like before ever burgeoning controls and Health & Safety Regulations took away much of the onus for common sense and personal safety from the individual and in so doing opened the door for the rapidly-spreading compensation culture.

In Malta, like many other countries around the world, everyday operation of the transport network still relies on the professionalism of its bus drivers and the nous of their passengers. Whether or not that produces more or less incidents/accidents per hundred thousand passenger journeys than here in the United Kingdom I cannot say, but it is immediately obvious that people of all ages act responsibly and that life is the better for it. It is also noteworthy that despite the

age of the vehicles, up to 50 years in many cases, breakdowns are uncommon. During five weeks of fairly intensive bus travel spread over five holidays spanning 13 years, I have seen only two broken down buses from a fleet of 500 plus machines, many of which would be very much at home in a UK preservation rally or vintage running day. I believe this speaks volumes for the standard of maintenance.

Whilst the actual condition of the bodywork of these veterans may sometimes be considered to be quite another matter I have no hesitation in recommending anyone to go and enjoy the experience, and the wonderful sunshine! As always some pre-planning will reap benefits and a handy pocket guide book published by the AA may be found useful. On arrival take the earliest opportunity to change a fairly large denomination note, buying a beer or a coffee, so that you have some change. A seven day bus ticket is a good investment but the machines which dispense these, in Sliema, Valletta and elsewhere, have their foibles like all vending machines. Try wherever possible to put the correct money in, since change may not always be in the local currency!

An early visit to the Tourist Information Centre should be a must. The one in Valletta is located in the parade of shops in Freedom Square at the head of Republic Street, immediately through the arch of the City Gate, and on the right hand side. The views from the road over the Gate should not be missed. From many year's personal experience the Cafe Royale, diagonally opposite the TI at the corner of Ordnance Street, can be relied on to serve excellent food and drinks. Another, new, refeshment stop is the terrace alongside the Lower Barracca Gardens, where, again the food, drink and service are excellent and the view of the harbour is absolutely unrivalled. Public toilets are not always easy to find but the latter stop boasts excellent facilities with disabled access – something quite rare at present.

A free bus timetable in the form of an A4 sheet of paper, with accompanying list of routes and map, can be obtained from the inspectors' kiosks in Sliema and Valletta and is essential for journey planning. There is also a more up-market version which can be purchased, and makes a good souvenir of your visit. Finally, be prepared to be asked to change vehicles in the Valletta bus station when you have just got settled in a seat in the vehicle you have been looking for all day!

Opposite: A varied scene in the bus station by Valletta's Triton fountain in late January 1990, with bright sun and a temperature of around 20°C making for a very pleasant break from the UK winter snows. The green livery, introduced in 1977, would remain in use until 1995. The temporary flag poles are ready for the festival of St Paul, celebrated the first week in February every year, and commemorating his ship being wrecked on the island *en route* to Rome for his trial in AD 60. [DSH]

Right: The port of Valletta is host to many of the liners which cruise the Mediterranean; the Upper Barracca Gardens provide a splendid viewpoint, and somewhere to sit in the shade whilst having a break from watching the buses! Here *Island Escape* is seen leaving Malta to continue its journeys at the end of October 2003. Even at that time of the year the temperature was in the 'eighties whilst the photograph shows the familiar blue skies and bright sunshine for which the island is renowned. In the background Fort Ricasoll keeps silent watch over the entrance to the Grand Harbour. [JAS]

The bus station at Porta Reale in Valletta will be a natural starting point for most bus journeys and any serious photography. This commercial postcard, taken over the top of the city gate, gives a splendid view looking out to Floriana.

The card was produced sometime in the 1980s and shows a selection of vehicle types largely unchanged for another decade. What would change, however, was the entrance positions as one-man-operation came into force; the centre entrances were moved one bay forward, a small job for the adaptable Maltese craftsmen who built, rebuilt and maintained these venerable vehicles.

Up until 1931 the Malta railway had used this area as its terminus; there was also a three-route electric tramway using open-top four-wheel tramcars which operated from here between 1905 and its closure. The central fountain, the Triton Fountain, was erected in the late 1950s.

courtesy : Perfecta Advertising Ltd, Malta.

PUBLISHER'S NOTE

Whilst every care has been taken in the compilation of this book, events are changing very quickly on the island and the publishers regret that they cannot be held responsible for any inaccurate information, which is offered in good faith. The opinions expressed are those of the author who has no connection with any of the eating establishments mentioned other than being a satisfied customer.

Malta Buses – A Potted History

Given the Colonial influence, it is perhaps not surprising that when the first motor buses were introduced nearly one hundred years ago they were British, being four Thornycroft double-deckers with seating for 36 which commenced running in 1905, coincidentally the year the electric trams began operation. In 1920 the Maltese-owned British Motor Company was formed and they utilised ex-war department vehicles, again reflecting practice in Great Britain. By 1922 about 50 two-ton vehicles were in use, with seats for 14-16 passengers, the first scheduled bus service having been introduced the year before between Valletta and Sliema.

Subsequently additional chassis were introduced, the wooden bodies being built by local craftsmen so that fleet sizes could be expanded rapidly such that by 1930 when the original licensing system ceased the number of route buses totalled about 500. The exception to the policy of operating locally built lightweight bodies (termed 'matchbox' bodies by some) was the BMC, which by then

had been bought by Overseas Motor Transport, a company under the control of Commander Hare of Devon Motor Transport. It was the only foreign organisation running buses in Malta and tended to prefer imported chassis with more substantial bodies on them; consequently its fares tended to be higher. By this time the government was becoming concerned about the confrontation between the two parties and also the safety implications, but appeared reluctant to act for fear of being accused of 'taking sides'.

Nevertheless new regulations were published during 1929 which came into force the following year, introducing amongst other features annual testing of vehicles. However, the middle of 1930 saw the constitution suspended and it fell to the Island's Governor (probably to the relief of the government!) to announce the appointment of a committee to enquire into and report on the motor bus service, it already having been decided to close the railway. Even before their report was issued, the issuing of additional licences ceased, and the recommendations that were published before the end of that year came into effect

in 1931 under the aegis of the newly created Traffic Control Board, at the time when the British Road Traffic Act of 1930 was still being finalised, and anticipating many of its forthcoming requirements. Nineteen thirty-one was a significant year, for 31st March saw the closure of the railway which coincided with the introduction of further regulatory measures. Owners had until July that year to comply with the new regulations or forfeit their licences in this time of upheaval.

The new arrangements, which saw the consolidation of operations into eleven routes, each identified by a unique colour, did not appear to suit the owners of the BMC who almost immediately sold their interest to Joseph Gasan and withdrew their buses to Egypt. The chronic problems brought about by the Second World War led to suggestions, not for the first time, that all buses be amalgamated into a single organisation, but this proposal was not proceeded with. Mr Gasan continued to expand such that by the immediate post-war period he owned 115 licences. It is believed that initially he obtained military Ford

When Peter Trevaskis was on Malta fifty years ago he was able to photograph the changing scene as the oldest of the pre-war buses were replaced by the new Fordsons, the various combinations of Bedford SBs, and the rebuilds of many wartime chassis whose use as the basis of a bus could only come about on Malta. A Reo is seen filling up at the refuelling point which still exists in the Valletta bus park today; its body is the pre-war standard type. A variety of more recent additions to the fleet can be seen in the distance. The fountain and new bus terminal, pictured opposite by Scott Hellewell, have yet to be built.

V8 chassis, fitted with Wayne body kits from Canada but subsequently he imported new Ford Thames chassis and had some fitted with bodies built by Joseph Aquilina. However, by 1955 he had sold his buses and the situation had reverted to its origins, mainly of single bus ownership.

The same year, 1955, saw the Traffic Control Board redistribute buses into 21 routes for Malta and one for Gozo. To this day the buses on Gozo retain the red and grey livery allocated at that time. Visitors to Gozo will notice that, in general, the vehicles on that island demonstrate less variety but are kept in somewhat better condition than the oldest Malta buses, perhaps reflecting their use as private hire vehicles.

A change of Government in 1971 foreshadowed further changes to the operation of Malta's buses. Like many alterations in Malta this reorganisation did not happen overnight and it was not until 1977 that the full range of these changes was implemented. Firstly, as a condition for obtaining an increase in fares, the bus owners accepted that a degree of amalgamation would take place.

From 1973 buses were merged into three groups (as a prelude to the formation of a single company from 1975). The first, largely serving the east of Malta, were painted spray green; the second, serving Sliema, were white with a blue band, whilst the third, generally serving the south and west, were red.

At this time the traditional destination display arrangements were replaced by numbers inserted into metal boxes in the windscreens, whilst the route numbers, the highest of which had previously only been route 21, were expanded and reached up to 94. There was also an increase in the number of services operating on nearby Gozo.

The amalgamation into a single company eventually took place in late 1977 and nine owners were elected

This veteran Ford had little time left when seen in August 1954, bound for the Custom House, Marsa. Unusually, it sports a front entrance.

Bedford lovers will recognise this one by the tyres — a QL four-wheel drive high chassis vehicle, rebuilt as a bus. It was eventually replaced by an AEC Mercury!

to manage the new company to be known as the Malta Bus Company. All buses were now painted green. Two years later the Government authorised the use of buses without a conductor. The 1980's were epitomised by the introduction of around 250 vehicles imported from the United Kingdom, which could be divided into four groups. In typical Maltese fashion, the first actually entered service during a strike period! These formed some of over 50 AEC Swifts which were purchased by the Government from London Transport. The second and third groups were 15 Bristol LH and 7 Leyland Tiger Cubs respectively, whilst the largest group comprised around 170 vehicles of Bedford and Ford manufacture with Plaxton or Duple bodies. Subsequent purchases of similar Plaxton and Duple coaches, some of which were used as route buses and others as unscheduled vehicles, brought the eventual total to around 240. This was a remarkable degree of standardisation, representing almost half the route buses, which nevertheless were quite unsuited to the purpose since the large glazed areas in these British coaches were far from ideal for Maltese operation. Incredibly, it was not until 1995 that it was agreed that the sealed windows could be replaced with sliders.

In 1989 a Public Transport Authority was established by Act of Parliament, and the policies

which are currently being implemented were developed. In 1995 the route buses colour was changed to the present yellow and orange, and plans for the new fleet of low floor buses were formulated. Five sample vehicles, illustrated on pages 65-67, were tested but not considered ideal although all remain in service. Further thinking, probably influenced by the desire to join the EU, resulted in the specification being upgraded – to Euro3 Level emissions for example. A more intensive utilisation of vehicles was also envisaged, which would result in a total fleet of c300 buses, and provide the opportunity to scrap the worst of the earlier vehicles.

It was also anticipated that the 'vehicle-day' would be 16 hours requiring two drivers each to work 8 hour shifts. This change in practice would eliminate the unique Maltese method of operation, dating back to 1931, whereby drivers and their buses worked on a day-on day-off basis. Whilst the peak requirement of around 254 vehicles currently requires an island fleet of some 508 buses it seems clear that future arrangements will reflect the cost of new vehicles and the combined investment from owner/Government, and it is therefore unlikely that the new vehicles will be allowed to stand idle.

Whatever the future holds it seems clear that the Malta bus scene will continue to offer much of interest to visitor, commuter and enthusiast alike. As a testimony to engineering expertise and ingenuity, long may it continue to do so.

If the QL, opposite, was unusual the International seen facing lower right was equally so. It had been a fire engine during the Second World War but now sported a smart SB type body when seen at Birkirkara. It was already over 20 years since trains had stopped here but this bus was still operating in 2002. The white-painted private hire bus, seen right, is indeed a Bedford SB, with Brincat bodywork. It is seen in East Street Valletta between duties. The Maltese balconies form an appropriate backdrop, whilst someone is busy replacing floor timbers in the house alongside. Renumbered as Y-0910 No. 4873 lasted until the influx of Plaxton and Duple coaches in the mid 1980s. [Peter Trevaskis – all four illustrations]

These next four colour shots show some of the vehicles which Venture's Ian Stubbs photographed in 1978. Some lasted another 25 years, whilst others were replaced much sooner. Others again were merely rebuilt, though the term 'mere rebuild' is a Maltese euphemism – 'anything goes' might be more accurate. Trying to identify the vehicles gives an indication of just how much work has gone into converting some of these machines, but just exactly what the starting point was can be almost impossible to determine. In this view the Bedford OB, 2415, carries a Schembri body. Similar OBs were still in service in 2003 but many other normal-control vehicles (where the driver sits behind the engine, not alongside it) had been converted by major rebuilding. The vehicle alongside, 2586, will have been a conversion, but just what was converted and by whom or when is uncertain. The use of existing components ranging from windscreens to complete fronts can make identification difficult; the badging and lettering is very often a good guide as to what the vehicle is not!

Less enigmatic is the Dodge shown in this illustration. Number 3355 carries bodywork by Aquilina, and became number 0778 in the renumbering and tidying up scheme of 1979-80 when registrations were reallocated from the recently adopted A- series to the Y- series seen in the next period, from page 10. Clearly a member of the post-war make-do-and-mend era this worthy bus illustrates many interesting features. The chassis is most likely to have been recovered from the military after the end of the war. The centre entrance bodywork has been mentioned previously; the small windscreen glasses are notable where many later designs would have external visors to cut down unwanted sunlight.

Note that sliding saloon windows are fitted, and that there appears to be no door – still everyday practice on most of the older bodies. The side route numerals are also noteworthy; by 1990 when the author visited the island these were no longer displayed but at that time there were rear route number displays. In every case the present-day card or perspex numbers were used. [IS both]

Two examples of major conversions are shown on this page. By good fortune both are illustrated in *The Malta Buses*, the history of the buses on the island and an invaluable and instructive work. Number 0338 is a pre-World War 2 Diamond machine, having originally been built to normal control configuration. It was later rebuilt to forward control, as shown, and is believed to have lasted in service in this form until the mid-sixties. The small windscreen glasses referred to previously can be seen again on this page and once again the disused aperture confirms that destination displays had been used, before being replaced by route numbers.

Below left is number 2981, hardly the most elegant design seen so far, but perhaps one of the more interesting. This operator-built body sits on a Leyland Hippo (lorry) chassis; the chrome grille is a later addition and the bus originally ran with its instantly recognisable Leyland radiator proudly facing the world. Modernisation crept in later, neatly disguising its origins. The date of its demise is uncertain, but when built by Leyland Motors it would have looked similar to the Hippo illustrated below from the Leyland archives. The third axle, left over after the conversion, would doubtless have come in useful for another project! The rugged construction of this type of chassis was ideal for the bad roads on the island, and convinced the owner drivers that only chassis from such heavyweight machines were really suitable for their needs. [IS; Leyland Motors]

This magnificent Dodge, bodied by Aquilina was one of the gems from the author's January 1990 visit – yes this is winter sunshine. Note that the numeric registrations have now been replaced by a Y- prefixed series (see the note below). The plates were embossed metal, painted red as seen here, with black lettering – the ideal combination for difficult reading and poor photography! As the black wore off the plates became even more difficult to read. Some appear to have been painted orange, just slightly easier to read. Y-0402 was photographed waiting to come on service into the bus station, opposite, and then again between journeys in the bus park, right. The darker green 'snout' enhances the already evocative appearance. Perhaps it needs to be mentioned that the Dodge was in normal all-day service on the long route 49 to the Gozo ferry mentioned later.

The reflections from the windows on the road opposite give an indication how polished the surface becomes, when it is not potholed. It is immediately noticeable how much slower and more carefully the drivers handle their steeds after a shower of rain. The narrow saloon window effect is caused by the sun catching the overlap of the sliding glass, closer examination will reveal that there are seven pillars behind the driver's door. The badging and other embellishment is attractive but fairly restrained and this is just one of many examples of a bus which would have been snapped up for a UK museum had that been possible. Until 2000 it had not been permissible to export a bus from Malta; only a handful have so far escaped since the ban was relaxed. This is a tragedy for some of the fine machines illustrated in these pages could have been found homes in museums across the world where they would have reminded people of happy times on the island, and generated a wish to return. There is now talk of a bus museum being set up in Malta and we can only hope other gems such as this will survive to be included. [JAS both]

MALTESE REGISTRATION NUMBERS

Until 1979 buses on Malta and Gozo carried a numeric identification, this being shown on a metal plate attached to the front and rear of each vehicle.

During 1979-80 this system was replaced by the use of a prefix letter, originally A but soon replaced by Y. This letter was then also used for all PSVs, taxis, private hire cars, unscheduled buses and minibuses. The old numbers, running randomly from 1– c. 8804 were replaced by Y-0300 to Y-0807 for the Route buses on Malta and Y-0808 to Y-0835 for those on Gozo.

In 1995 the present system was introduced, coinciding with the present livery. Photographs show that the changeover was not achieved overnight.

The Y series was replaced by DBY 300-470, EBY 471-640 and FBY 641-807, except for a Solaris introduced in 2002 which carries EBY 433.

Buses on Gozo carry FBY 001-079.

More nostalgia with this selection of venerable British machines of yesteryear. The larger view of splendid Ford Thames Y-0313 shows off its still straight waistrail and roofline whilst below we see Y-0399, Bedford OB Y-0781, and also note the venerable Thornycroft Sturdy Y-0382 with its distinctive snout, seen again on page 25.

And what of the replacements for this brave quartet? Y-0313 was replaced by a Solaris from Poland, Y-0399 by a locally bodied MAN, and Y-0781 by a BMC Maltese Falcon from Turkey. And the Thornycroft? Its connection to the island's very first buses in 1905 was severed when a Chinese King Long ousted it in 2003. A collective sad testimony to the state of the British manufacturing industry in the 21st century, many would argue. [JAS all]

Looking over the bonnet of Bedford OB 'St Mary', Y-0781. From its spot in the shade we can see the Sliema departure platforms with a selection of vehicles; prominent in the centre is the Sammut-bodied Mercedes Y-0794, partly hiding an ex-London Swift, with a Plaxton Supreme alongside and finally a pair of Bedfords. This is start of the slope used for clutch starts by many of the buses departing from this side of the bus station.

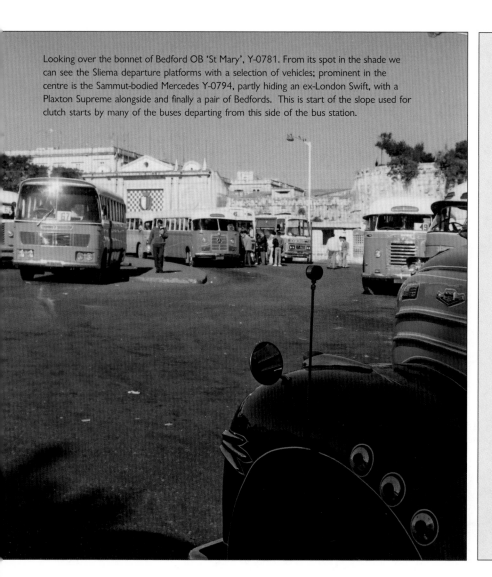

Expressions of the driver's faith will often be found in and around his bus; the more restrained Latin verses of earlier days are giving way to a more direct affirmation in some instances, as below. [JAS all three]

A selection of Bedfords together with a Kew built Dodge – or at least that's how they are believed to have started life. The splendid pair opposite, standing by the Triton fountain, are both working the 62 route to Sliema and Paceville; Y-0687 takes a breather whilst Y-0381 disgorges yet another load of passengers for the Sunday market. And when they go back they'll have to hang on to all their bags of purchases as they try to keep their balance while strap hanging through the journey! Both carry Brincat bodywork, the former on an SB chassis and the latter on a dockyard conversion. Y-0687, later registered as EBY 607, was replaced by a BMC Maltese Falcon in 2003.

Waiting by the despatcher's office, this page upper, is Y-0499, a Casha bodied Bedford SBO working the 18 route to Zabbar. The carillon from the town's church is one of many on the island which form a part of the ambience. Route 18 is another of the high intensity services, in this case during rush hour no frequency is stated – buses just run as often as required to move the crowds. Some of us older Brits can remember those days back in the UK – something to do with providing a service as I recall it.

In the lower view Y-0749 could at first sight be another Bedford; it is in fact an AEC as its badge rightly states, but an AEC Mercury lorry chassis bodied by Debono. Note that the driver's door has been removed for the summer, allowing some much-needed air to circulate through the bus, helping to refresh the driver and his passengers alike. [DSH lower right; others JAS]

The Triton fountain provides a grandstand, panoramic view, with tiered seating and the opportunity to have a quick refreshing shower when the wind suddenly swings round in the opposite direction. It forms a natural meeting point every bit as good as 'below the clock at Waterloo station' once was.

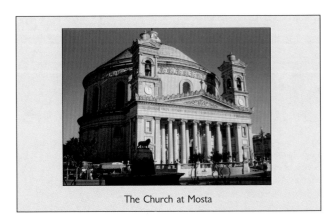

The Church at Mosta

Route 49, travelling from Valletta in the south east to Cirkewwa for the Gozo ferry in the north west, is the longest on the island with a journey time of 70 minutes. At peak times during Monday to Saturday the frequency becomes every 7½ minutes, but on Sunday it is further augmented as required. Thus there may be in excess of 20 vehicles on the service on Sundays. One of the principal points of interest on the route is Mosta, and the church there should not be missed. It has one of the largest unsupported domes in Europe, and is well worth a visit by anyone in the area to see such a gem in just a small town in Malta. Mosta is also home to Paramount Garage, one of the larger operators of buses and coaches; their fleet includes the four Dennis Darts from the 1997 advance low-floor demonstrators in addition to a selection of coaches and minicoaches.

Here Barbara-bodied Bedford SB Y-0709, probably dating from the mid-fifties but rebuilt in 1959, speeds round the corner by the church, heading back to Valletta.

On the facing page (upper) Y-0381, a Brincat-bodied Bedford whose chassis was rebuilt in the dockyard waits its turn to join the Sunday procession on the 49. Note that unlike many of these bodies this one has a door in the forward entrance. Standing alongside is Y-0671, originally a Bedford OB and beautifully illustrated in *The Malta Buses* both in original condition and later as shown here after being rebuilt to forward control by Barbara. It was replaced by a Maltese Falcon in 2003. Note that by 1990 side destination numbers had been replaced by rear ones as in the lower photograph, showing Y-0672, another dockyard conversion also with Brincat bodywork. The rear fin styling which is common to several buses has echoes of the British Ford Classic saloon of the time. [JAS all]

Typical of the ornamentation which abounds on the Maltese buses – horse shoes, mottoes and plenty of very clever paintbrush work; the new buses will doubtless follow suit before too long. [JAS all]

Early morning spruce-up for the buses at Sliema ferry terminus; the morning mist gives the drivers a head start on cleaning the windows with a wash leather. Although it is only seven o'clock on a January morning the sun is already strong as the right hand views, taken at the same time, demonstrate. Y-0317, later DBY 317, seen in the upper views, is another Bedford SB with Barbara bodywork; the louvres above the side windows are noteworthy. The 61 is one of the several routes from Sliema to Valletta's City Gate – *aka* Porta Royale – bus terminus.

New in 1962 this body shows its Duple ancestry at the rear with what are almost certainly back screens from the Super Vega body range of the late 'fifties. The earlier rear, possibly also using Duple components from the original body, belongs to an earlier Bedford, again rebuilt by Barbara some time later in its career. Its origin is reputed to be unknown; later registered as FBY 781 it became another victim when the Falcons swooped down in 2003.

The saplings in these views, here supported by more robust trunks, have formed a fine line of mature trees, as can be seen in later pictures in this book. This area is the departure point for several bus services, including the (intentional) vintage one. It is also one of the places to buy weekly tickets, or to take a harbour cruise with Captain Morgan. A particularly satisfying and inexpensive way to enjoy the harbour crossing is to walk from Republic Street down Old Theatre Street to the ferry terminal in Valletta, passing the Anglican cathedral before walking down the long flight of stone steps, and then catching the ferry back to this point. [JAS all]

Some of the Bedford conversions leave no doubt as to their origins; here yet another SB navigates the roundabout at Msida. Situated at the end of Sliema creek, where the marina finishes, this is a pleasant spot to take a breather and watch the world go by. A seemingly never-ending procession of buses heading for Valletta pass here. War Memorial grounds with plenty of trees flank the road behind the photographer, there are also comfortable seats and benches in a sunken paved area and opposite, to the right in this view, is the Busy Bee café; frequented by the locals, which is always a good sign, this is another one not to be missed. Two bus stops, one just to the left behind the camera and the other some five minutes walk further towards Valletta, provide convenient boarding points.

The Schembri bodied dockyard conversion Y-0353, seen left, another of unknown ancestry, displays its externally attractive lines with unusual glass cantrail windows. Travelling in this when the sun is out could have been purgatory, even worse than the Dominants and Supremes, but the glass has been painted over and it does have the usual sliding windows in every bay to allow plenty of air to circulate. Note that St Michael has made his appearance amongst the saints on the island; perhaps in deference to local sensitivities the Marks and Spencer name later replaced this wording on the Sliema promenade frontage. [JAS all]

Is this a Duple Viceroy type front, but in a body by local bodybuilder Grech? The chassis is a Bedford SBG, ex-Ministry of Defence, and the bodywork presents a very smart looking conversion. Close examination will reveal that even these large panoramic windows are in fact full-depth half-sliders, absolutely essential in the Mediterranean heat. Y-0694, later FBY 694, stands ready for an early morning departure from Sliema ferry; once again the opening door is noteworthy.

An animal of a very different breed is seen above right, quite a wanderer in fact. Underneath its 36-seat Brincat body lurk the remains of a Bolton Corporation Leyland Titan TD5c of long ago. If the records are to be believed, and there is no reason to doubt them, this was once a double-decker bus operating in the Lancashire town close to the manufacturer, registered WH 9202 and one of a batch seen in the maker's illustration, built in 1937. Here it is registered Y-0801 before becoming FBY 801. It is interesting to speculate in what form it might have arrived in Malta; as a chassis or with its lower-deck only? Since Leyland's bus bodies were built in two halves it would have been easy to separate them and it seems most unlikely that it came over complete – unless anyone knows to the contrary? But see also page 50! Still in service in 2001 it finally bit the dust sometime in 2002/3, being replaced by a King Long. [JAS – two colour illustrations]

On an island where bus enthusiasts possibly outnumber the police at some times of the year, photographers have no cause for alarm from the constabulary despite the apparent impression to the contrary given in this view. Note the variety of transport: the local horse drawn karozzins, the white Mercedes taxis in the Y-series of registrations used by the buses, a locally registered car likely to be moved on or boxed in by the buses, and the buses themselves. This is a Sunday morning when the bus park is taken over by a huge open market, yet another thing not to be missed. Perhaps some of the components from the many recently scrapped buses may appear here for recycling, who knows? [JAS]

Maltese bus owners were proficient in the art of badge-engineering long before British Leyland and the rest thought of it. This splendidly presented OB, named St Mary and registered Y-0781, later FBY 781, shows just how much decoration can be applied – limited only by the owner's imagination and his ability to find suitable ironmongery. This vehicle shows distinct echoes of British narrow boat traditional paintwork; was the watering can used for topping up the radiator decorated to match, one wonders?

Photographed on the sea front at Sliema before breakfast the bus had just had its morning wash and brush up, leathering down, and interior swept clean ready for the day's madding crowds in an hour or two. Its condition is a credit to the owner-driver, a one-man-band whose pride in his steed is all-evident. That his reward was, by British standards, a pittance is a potent reminder that money is indeed not the be-all-and-end-all of life.

Later in the morning bus and camera were reunited at Porta Royale as the OB and its driver worked the 67 service as seen opposite. The eight-bay bodywork, seating 36 passengers, gives an indication of work carried out below decks in lengthening the chassis whilst the power unit will be decidedly more powerful than the original petrol engine fitted to the OBs at Hendon. [JAS all]

A trip around Valletta, or a part of it, in a karozzin is another experience which can be recommended. The smooth streets tax the horses on the steep climbs but a good guide will make it a memorable occasion.

Home from home on the bus is a truism for these one-man owner-drivers – at present (ie up to December 2003) they still work a 16 hour day and then have to maintain, fuel and clean their bus ready for the next duty. They decorate the vehicles to remind them of their loved ones, their faith, their favourite cars, pets or whatever, and this view is typical of the interior of many of the buses. Note the icons, motto, strap hangars and bell cords all jostling for space. In a devoutly Catholic country we are spared the page three girls.

A sign of changing times is hanging in the windscreen – as likely as not it will be badges of football clubs. Many of the younger drivers are exchanging their religious icons for more recognisable modern day paraphernalia. Football scarves, badges, programmes, miniature boots and the whole rigmarole often appear. Sometimes country-and-western, rock-and-roll or the Beatles memorabilia will feature.

In 1990 it was not uncommon to find a live canary in a cage keeping the driver company. Sadly this nostalgic scene is changing as the younger men get newer buses while the forthcoming regulations on driver's hours, which will mean more than one man will be responsible for taking each vehicle on the road, will probably also hasten the change. [JAS both]

Look out for the trotting carts which can be seen out around the island – on Sundays they race at the stadium at Marsa and a selection of buses from Valletta will take you there.

Still taxed until 2003, but the test disc is an old one
– for Y-0382 and last inspected in 1994 !

One foot hard down on the accelerator and the other even harder down on the horn as Y-0382, the Thornycroft Sturdy, roars round the corner at Msida. Brute force and experience come together and the car driver won't chance his arm unless he is very sure he can get out of the way. The squeal of tyres on the smooth roads is a constant reminder of these antics but in most instances it will be tyre spin on acceleration, rather than last minute braking. On one occasion on a changeover of driver on the road it was interesting to watch him being quickly guided through the controls for his first trip behind the wheel of a King Long – first the horn, then the radio, then the seat adjustment. Well what else could you need to know?

The venerable Thornycroft was withdrawn during 2003, one more of the old timers to be replaced by a King Long. First noted in service in 1948 it had given some 55 year's service, retaining its original appearance throughout. [JAS]

The
Interlopers

Malta had had to be self-reliant after the ravages of the Second World War. Indeed, its economy long before that had been based on hard work and thrift, but the devastation left after the continuous bombing meant that make-do-and-mend had to be the order of the day for several decades.

In public transport this translated into no imports of complete vehicles. In addition to the surviving pre-war bus fleet there was a selection of ex-military buses and lorries, many of which could be adapted by the skilled local craftsmen as has been seen in the photographs so far. Bedfords of all types abounded, with spares available, and bodybuilding provided local employment.

This state of affairs continued until the reorganisations of the late 'seventies when it was decided to allow some importation of (complete) second-hand British buses to take place. The amalgamations which had led to the formation of the single group in 1977 made such matters easier, but the police's concern over the by-then alarming state of some of the veterans finally won the day.

A deal was negotiated concerning the purchase of a number of former London Transport AEC Swifts. Unwanted and definitely unloved literally hundreds of them were parked on a disused airfield in Hertfordshire, England − there was nowhere else big enough − awaiting buyers. Since London Transport had made such a fuss about their 'unsuitability' perhaps it was not surprising prospective purchasers were slow in coming.

Around fifty-six of these vehicles duly came to the island, purchased by the Government, and presented a very great contrast in terms of engine layout (at the rear), doorway positions (two, one right at the front), transmission (automatic) and other items. Fortuitously for the Government, they arrived as a bus strike was about to take place and were pressed into emergency service. Their large capacity was to be most useful at this time.

When peace returned to the bus scene 40 were made available to the bus owners as replacements, and the remainder stayed in Government ownership. Some of the latter entered service with the Education Department, painted purple and white, as seen on page 28, whilst the others appeared in the then recently adopted green and white, suitably embellished and looking far smarter than they had ever done in the UK.

London Transport may have had problems with them, but happily managing without such vast resources the Maltese drivers soon had them in hand from their back street garages. Where there's a will there's a way, especially if you are using your own meagre financial resources. If double-decker operation had been permissible Maltese owner/drivers would no doubt also have shamed LT by equally successfully running a selection from the hundreds of prematurely cast-off DMS double-deckers also considered 'unsuitable' for operation in the UK capital.

As good as new − or better? Certainly better respected and cared for, Y-0662, the former London SM 33 is seen in Valletta in January 1990. [JAS]

Two of the former London Swifts showing just how much the appearance has been enhanced by the new frontal embellishment on Y-0589, originally SMS292, when compared to Y-0763, originally SM34. Note that on both vehicles the former centre doorway has been removed and panelled over. The vehicle's strength was its main virtue.

The registration plates are worthy of note; whilst Y-0589, seen loading in this 1992 view at Valletta bus station has a red background plate, Y-0763 nearer the camera clearly carries an orange plate. Notice also the Duple 'cheesecutter' moulding on the upgraded vehicle, in addition to the use of roller blinds for destination numbers. Is the driver of the 35 contemplating bringing his vehicle up to the same standard as he sits watching it load, we wonder? If so he has some way to go!

In later life most of these ex-London vehicles would be given some substantial rebuilds, including centrally mounted vertical engines which required the whole floor level to be raised. The rails on the seat backs will be the clue to this action. One vehicle has even been converted to underfloor-engine configuration. Transmission lines and gearboxes have also had radical attention after years of hard slog on the Maltese roads. [DSH]

In this view what is believed to be Y-0525 has also been embellished with what could well be a Duple Dominant side moulding. Again the vehicle is well presented and a credit to its owner. Note that both vehicles on this page have roller blind numbers in the original destination boxes, and that in line with those used in the windscreens they are black on white, opposite to accepted UK practice. [JAS]

27

The Ministry of Education has a fleet of vehicles which it uses for school transport. When the former London Transport AEC Swifts were purchased by the Maltese Government in 1970 several of these were allocated to this fleet, being then painted in the purple and white livery applied to all its vehicles. They were not rebuilt in the manner of the route buses, the second doorway being left intact, for example. Others of these Swifts were later sold to private operators, to be used as route buses, as seen in the previous pages. Some remained in Government ownership, but were apparently unused.

Seen at Floriana in January 1990, M 1523, upper left, was originally EGN269J – SMS 269. This vehicle subsequently operated on Gozo and was later renumbered GVH 139 in a new series of registration numbers. An example of this series is seen upper right in the Valletta bus park as GVH 140, earlier being M 1522 and before that, originally, EGN 259J as SMS 259, when in London.

Also in the Education fleet is a rather unusual Fiat, GVH 131, seen lower left; again the 47-seat body by Borsani is fitted with two doors but of the coach variety which open outwards. In the background is another Ministry vehicle, a Plaxton Supreme coach on a Bedford chassis, possibly one fitted with a lift for the disabled.

By the time these views were taken in 1990 the invasion had taken place and in addition to Swifts there were also Bristol LHs from Western National and Crosville Motor Services, in addition to Duple Dominants and Plaxton Surpremes from various UK operators. Examples can be seen here, still with the original fixed side windows. There was, of course, no air conditioning in these vehicles.

Apparently, for some considerable time it was not permissible to change these for opening windows, and the author has a vivid memory of roasting inside one at Luqa airport whilst waiting to be taken to the hotel in Sliema, and that was in January. The idea of travelling in them in the summer, packed with standing passengers, doesn't bear thinking about.

Y-0785, seen right, was formerly operated by Blackburn Corporation, a close neighbour of Bolton which was mentioned earlier. Later registered as FBY 785 it is a Leyland underfloor-engined Tiger Cub, still carrying its original East Lancashire Coachbuilders bodywork, built in its home town. New in 1967 as Blackburn's number 12 it operated for some 14 years before being purchased by CarmeloVella, a Mosta operator. Other similar vehicles were purchased from the same source at the same time and appear later in the book. [JAS both]

The banner in the windscreen confirms that this is a Leyland-engined Bristol LH, with the standard NBC style Eastern Coach Works body, built at Lowestoft.

Perhaps more interesting in this classic shot is the driver's posture as he gives his steed the gun as they speed round the corner in Mosta – jay walkers beware! Closer examination of his hands will be interesting: right hand holding the knob bolted to the steering wheel's rim, left hand on his knee. Driving with one hand in this fashion is commonplace, even on the tight bends on the hills. Gear changes are often accomplished on the older vehicles without using the clutch, and watching these drivers at work is truly an education. Crashing gears are almost unknown, as is the use of the starter motor unless the vehicle is pointing uphill! The one essential is a good, loud, two-tone horn – the louder the better – and many of these roof mounted appurtenances can be seen fixed above the driver in the photographs in this book.

A quieter moment for fellow Bristol Y-0544, later EBY 544, but perhaps remembered by some enthusiasts as once being GDV460N when it operated as Western National's number 1611. The short length and 45-seat capacity is just right for Malta but it will be a very hot ride with only three small sliding windows each side for the passengers – and this is January. This was, however, infinitely better than would be provided in the huge influx of fixed-window Dominants and Supremes which would soon arrive. [JAS both]

GOZO INTERLUDE

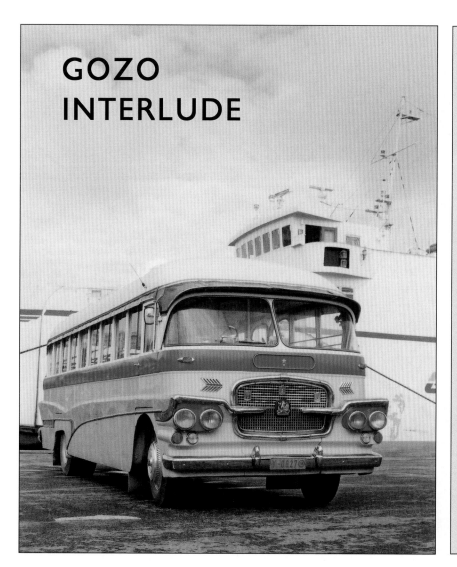

The short crossing to Gozo from Malta's Cirkewwa terminal gives a view of Comino, the third of the island trio, which is situated between Malta and Gozo. There is no public transport on Comino, and only a handful of people live there. The upgrading of the ferries from that shown in the main picture to the ones above and below has shortened the journey time and offers improved on-board facilities. A selection of Gozo buses and coaches will usually be awaiting the boat's arrival at Mgarr. [JAS left; RGR; PG]

The silver grey and maroon livery applied to the buses on Gozo has given them a touch of class ever since it was first introduced in 1955.

Bedford SB Y-0827, seen on page 31 waiting at the ferry terminal, and opposite some years later re-registered in the current system as FBY 015, looks smart despite its advancing years.

Bodied by Zammit and dating from around 1962, it will perform route bus duties, unscheduled work and school runs during the course of its weekly routines. It was originally a route bus on Malta, working the Birkirkara service before the amalgamation, and carrying the number 3095. Later it became A-3095, Y-1528, Y-0827 and finally FBY 015 when photographed in Victoria.

On this page another Bedford, Y-0825, carrying bodywork by Aquilina, is seen in the capital Victoria – formerly Rabat – between duties. At first glance it could be just another Duple-bodied SB, indicating how closely the Maltese bodybuilders followed the lines of the British classic design. This vehicle became FBY 026. Both the Y-series red registration plated photographs were taken in 1990, whilst FBY 015 was shot in 2001. [JAS all three]

There are many types of Bedford chassis in use on the two islands but this one was apparently a lorry in its previous life. Rebuilt with bodywork by Aquilina around 1956 it was photographed at Xlendi terminus in 2002. [RGR]

Plaxton Paramount bodywork is carried by the Bedford YNT seen opposite. New in 1987 the coach put in ten year's service in the UK before being purchased for service on Gozo. It is seen in 1999 on a private hire working for Newmarket Holidays. [JAS]

This ERF coach, registered FBY 006, with Marshall bodywork, was supplied to Bonnici Coaches in 1997 as a demonstrator. Marshall SPV was running into financial problems back in the UK and there was thus no possibility of any further progress with this combination. The vehicle, in common with all others operating on the islands at that time, has a very high floor line and the author remembers that on the occasion of this photograph several members of the party found boarding and alighting quite difficult. The doorway behind the coach leads to a spring which, feeding into a large stone basin, is used by local housewives as a public wash house for the daily or weekly laundry. [JAS]

A very different kind af coach, photographed by Paul Wigan in Victoria Bus Station on the occasion of the Modelstone Bus Club's October 2003 visit. Originally a 1953 Leyland Royal Tiger with Leyland centre-entrance 41-seat coach body, registered FCK402, it was rebodied when it came to Malta in June 1973.

After being withdrawn from front-line service by Ribble, where it would have worked, amongst other services, the prestigious London and Glasgow routes, it passed to Wimpey for use as staff transport; along with many other vehicles it was too good to scrap but no longer in the vanguard of current fashion for coach use and, with its high floor and centre entrance, was unsuitable for bus work. Neither of these aspects mattered to contractors, of course.

Close examination by two of the MBC group who are Ribble Preservationists confirmed that it retains its original Leyland O.600 engine. It is now registered FBY 037, and was rebodied by Schembri in 1973. It was earlier registered Y-0815, Y-1516, A-2070 and 2070 for those who may wish to trace its lineage. When this photograph was taken it was one of four former Ribble vehicles still operating on Malta and Gozo. Another is seen on page 45. [PW]

A busy scene as passengers board one of the waiting coaches for the trip to Victoria Bus Station in Gozo's capital. Formerly known as Rabat the town is nowadays called Victoria, as previously mentioned. Note that to assist intending passengers both the destination and the fare are clearly displayed in the windscreen of the Duple Dominant coach, alongside the route number.

The access to the ferry's car decks is clearly visible on both vessels. A third ferry is normally berthed in Valletta, in reserve. During the crossing when two boats are in use they will pass each other quite close, midway between Malta and Gozo, port to port as is usual, providing a good photo opportunity for those on deck. [RGR]

1995 – and a new livery

The appearance of the vehicles in the spray green and white livery, reflecting the former Cottonera, Calkara route colours, when changed to yellow and white with an orange band, the livery of the Siggiewi, Zebugg, Qormi routes, is seen in these four views. Ford ET7 number 159, later DBY 313, compares with EBY 537 whilst below, Y-0356, later DBY 356, a Chevrolet Debono, compares with DBY 381, a Dockyard-Bedford Brincat. [IS; JAS; DSH; RGR]

One among many of the particularly interesting survivors is Y-0368, later DBY 368, as seen in the four views on this page. A Reo Speedwagon of early 'thirties vintage it might have looked similar to the preserved example − restored to original condition − shown lower right at a UK rally in 2001. After rebuilding to normal control the Malta vehicle assumed its present appearance and progressed, with the rest of the fleet, from green to yellow. Perkins on the rear panel and on the radiator shell indicates the engine make, as ever. The latest photograph, top right, was taken in November 2003 when the bus had recently been splendidly repainted, yet again during its long life!
[DSH two left views; JAS two right]

MEANWHILE – BACK ON MALTA

The number of Bedford OBs in service is rapidly declining, but one of the magnificent survivors is seen facing. Photographed in a shady spot in Valletta bus station it carries a Brincat body dating it into service to December 1959. The decoration applied to the body is in the best traditions of Maltese art.

The side advert for Jacob's coffee is noteworthy, many vehicles which carry adverts in this position are promoting the use of public transport generally, or by showing ticket prices, night service details and the like.

The orange band, coinciding with the typical waistrail, is also noteworthy. It appears to be common to almost all locally built bodies from whatever source. Reference to the earliest pictures in this book, dating from the mid-fifties, confirms that this feature, which until very recently was still used, goes back at least that far. It would be interesting to know how this came about, whether this is a wooden rail, whether there is one common source for the material and how it came to be adopted as a standard. [DSH]

FBY 704, an Austin K4 with Brincat body, seen below waiting by the fountain, was new in Coronation Year, 1953. Austins were never very common in Malta; during the 1980s there were approximately half a dozen but by the mid 1990s FBY 704 was the sole survivor. Once owned by Mario Pio Camilleri of Mosta, by 2003 this fifty-year old vehicle was being operated by Joseph Ellul of Mqabba. [JAS]

A wash and brush up for Casha-bodied Fordson DBY 399 ready for the next day's work. In the background the selection includes former London Transport and Blackburn vehicles. Built in 1957, this bonnetted veteran was photographed in April 2002. [AWD]

This splendid Fordson ET7 had just been overhauled and repainted when photographed in Sliema in 2002. The interior finish matched the outward appearance and the vehicle was a credit to its owner. If the idea of running some of the older vehicles on the new hop-on hop-off Tourist Routes comes to fruition gems such as this will certainly keep the Malta bus scene alive. [JAS]

Some of the bonnetted vehicles, badged as Chevrolets and Dodges, true to form, are neither. This Gasan-bodied example is a Ford V8 normal-control model, photographed in 2002. EBY 636 entered service in 1945; at that time Ford was the most numerous chassis type on the island, over 100 being in service in 1948. [DSH]

Whilst some vehicles hide their light beneath their full-fronted bodywork, others are always instantly recognisable. One of the latter was, until its withdrawal, the Magirus Deutz, DBY 421. New in 1956, and bodied by Debono, its distinctive bonnet meant it was always easy to spot from afar. It was replaced by a King Long in 2003. [PW]

On the other hand, DBY 458 seen below left, and FBY 674, below right, could be almost anything. They are, in fact, almost bed-fellows from a former existence.

DBY 458, formerly DRN703, is another of the ex-Ribble Royal Tigers enjoying a second life. Rebodied by Aquilina around 1972 it is seen here in April 2002 about to perform another circuit of the number 1 route. It was the first of Ribble's new Leyland-bodied coach fleet when delivered as No. 781 in 1951. There were 145 of the classic design in the fleet, delivered between 1951 and 1953, and they were destined to be Ribble's last Leyland bodies.

FBY 674, an AEC Reliance, was formerly North Western's 847, RDB 847, an Alexander-bodied coach of 1961 which would almost certainly have worked into Manchester alongside the Ribble Royal Tiger. Now bodied by Ciantar it too is negotiating the roundabout at the end of The Mall as it leaves the environs of the bus station. [Both PW]

45

Left – One of the veterans waits to take a private party from a Msida hotel; the white board in the windscreen confirms that this bus is working a private hire, thus indicating it is an unscheduled bus and not a route bus – or at least it was when photographed on that particular day.

Sliema Strand is the location for DBY 309, a Bedford dockyard conversion bodied by Barbara around 1967, seen opposite working the popular 62 route to its terminus at Paceville. Note the four types of Maltese balconies: the traditional enclosed balcony towards the rear of the vehicle contrasts with the wrought iron ones on the second floor of what is now Marks & Spencer's building. Above the optician's shop is a very utilitarian example whilst the new apartments behind the rear of the bus show a typical modern Mediterranean seaside frontage.

The proliferation of loose wires hanging down represents another aspect of the Maltese scene which is being replaced; many areas have benefited from the removal of such unsightly electrical supplies as the general improvement of the area continues. Nowhere is this more apparent, perhaps, than along the other promenade heading towards St Julian's where newly constructed sun traps, with forms in the semi-circular outposts, sit comfortably amongst the reconstructed pavements with roadside flowerbeds. [JAS both]

Whilst the bonnetted buses perhaps have more charisma, the sheer number of buses of the types shown on this spread perhaps represent what to most people is a typical Malta bus. Three on the facing page were seen in the Valletta bus station whilst the fourth, with driver's door removed, was photographed at Mellieha. The opportunities for embellishment on these old buses are rarely wasted.

Facing upper left is EBY 536, a forward-control Dodge, presumably with a Leyland engine, bodied by Casha, whilst upper right DBY 434 is an Indiana chassis, dating from around 1938 and bodied by Aquilina in 1954. Both had originally been normal control vehicles. [JAS both]

The lower pictures illustrate two vehicles whose chassis came from the dockyard. Lower left is EBY 565, bodied by Gauci, on what was a 'new' chassis in 1962, probably a Perkins-engined Bedford rebuild. Just visible above the number plate on the original print can be seen the numbers 2590, being the vehicle's first registration. Lower right, DBY 308, has AEC running units and was bodied by Tonna. [JAS; DSH]

This page, right, DBY 398 is another dockyard chassis, this time with Brincat bodywork from around 1963. [JAS] Like FBY 752, below, a Diamond T with Aquilina bodywork from the end of 1950, it was photographed on Sliema Strand. [DSH]

Another numerical enigma? This is clearly FBY 801, which the records say is the former Bolton Corporation Leyland double-decker as seen on page 20. However it is clearly not the same body as carried by the then Y-0801 which became FBY 801. Or did it? Is this a different body on the same chassis, a completely different vehicle, or what? Whatever it is it makes an attractive picture in this view captured by Alan Drabble in April 1998.

Malta had a metre gauge railway until 1931. It had been opened in 1883 with just one line which ran from Valletta to Rabat. Sadly, virtually nothing remains today except for this partially restored coach standing on a couple of lengths of rail set to standard gauge, and the former station building here at Birkirkara (long since closed), behind the coach in this view. The grounds have been set out as gardens and the spot is a pleasant one in which to pass half an hour out of the sun. As always in Malta the local cats will join you for lunch!

The number 41, 42, 74 and 78 buses from Valletta terminate here at Birkirkara, as seen in the main illustration of EBY 639, a Federal chassis with Aquilina bodywork. When travelling from Valletta be sure to look out of the offside windows of the bus for an earlier form of transport near Birkirkara, the remains of the stone aqueduct which once carried water from the natural springs at Rabat down to Valletta.

A later view showing a King Long parked here gives an indication of the changing face of Malta's bus scene, see page 72. [AWD all three]

The term Route Bus crops up frequently as one looks into the use of Malta's buses; to the author's knowledge only one bus in recent times was actually so branded. FBY 736, a Bedford SB originally owned by the Royal Navy, now with Barbara 1973 bodywork, is seen here leaving the bus station on route 29 heading for Zejtun where Canchu Surpreme Travel, owners of three open-top double-deckers bodied by Eastern Coach Works, have their base.

A Route Bus would perhaps be better known in the UK as a Service Bus. In Malta it is used to distinguish the vehicle from an Unscheduled Bus, which may be a Route Bus on its 'Day Off', or a coach, as seen on page 70. When FBY 736 was not used on Scheduled Services, ie as a Route Bus, did the owner change the windscreen one wonders?! [JAS]

The three 'vintage' buses used for private hire and tours were originally built for Captain Morgan Tours. Now operated by Cancu Coaches they operate from Sliema Strand, two of the three normally being in use at any time. Their hard springing on the infamous potholed roads provides an interesting experience not recommended for those suffering from back problems. The chassis date from the 'twenties/ 'thirties with replica bodies built around 1990 – thus despite their appearance they are considerably younger than many buses still operating in every day service! [JAS both]

A quiet moment for three of the older buses at the terminus a few minutes walk below the stone gatewayed entrance to Mdina, the silent city. The centre vehicle, shown in more detail on the facing page, has just worked a private hire for the Modelstone Bus Club whose members visit the island each year to keep up-to-date with developments in the local transport network. It is flanked by a pair of Bedfords, the one on the left in this view, EBY 632, being another SB now carrying a local built Zammit body; the other, EBY 552, carries a Tonna body. Both vehicles' origins are apparently unknown. The wall, in the shade, provides a comfortable point to wait and watch the buses coming and going, whilst also providing a good view of approaching vehicles climbing the long hill as seen in the picture of an ex-London Transport AEC Swift on the next page. In the small illustration Peter Gascoine, founder of the Modelstone Bus Club, is seen being interviewed by Quaster Produktion for German Television in connection with a programme on the old buses, confirming the world-wide interest in Malta's transport. [JAS below, HB left]

Former London Transport Swift SMD 60, originally registered AML 60H, now EBY 576, climbs the long
hill to Mdina, gaining a tail of other vehicles in its wake. The lettering on the driver's side window records it,
correctly, as being an AEC Swift. The larger Marshall branding is wishful thinking; this is a Park Royal-bodied
example, but Marshall is still a name to be reckoned with on the Island. [JAS]

Three different aspects of Maltese Swifts: upper right FBY 723, with Metro-Cammell bodywork, formerly SMS 803, is a substantially rebuilt version with the high seating line, clearly visible, indicating a change from the original rear engine to a vertical unit under the floor which has been raised accordingly. The underfloor vertical engine configuration follows that of the later Bedford Y-range, of which over 200 can be found on the island. The transmission will doubtless also have been changed on the Swift. Over 50 Swifts were purchased by the Maltese Government, and in 2003 at least 33 of these were in use as route buses.

DBY 305, below, once a dual-door example and originally SMS 244, has had two major rebuilds whilst on Malta, the first during 1988 and the second between 1994 and 1998. Note it has gained a new front to its Park Royal bodywork. [JAS both]

Another Park Royal example, formerly SMS 232 but now DBY 380. There have been several vehicles with rear adverts, often for Nescafé coffee, covering the whole of the rear wall, as it is sometimes called, but this view shows one of the very few all-over Maltese advertising route buses when photographed in 2003. It carries normal livery on the front only. From the position of the seats it appears to have retained its rear engine. [PG]

Following the lifting of the ban on importing complete buses which had allowed the purchase of the ex-London Transport Swifts a small number of Bristol LHs arrived, mostly from former National Bus Company subsidiaries, and these introduced Eastern Coach Works bodies to the island. The vehicles are fitted with Leyland 400 series engines, accounting for the Leyland branding by some of their owners. Their 45 seat capacity is ideal for the route bus work they carry out and the opening windows offer some respite from the summer heat.

Note the Duple Dominant ribbed stainless steel moulding attached to this example, enhancing the already neat lines of the bodywork. Similar attachments have been made to some of the Swifts. In October 2003 there were 15 of these Bristol LH buses on Malta and one on Gozo, in addition to two Plaxton coach-bodied examples, one on each island.

EBY 520, originally a Crosville vehicle, is seen being scrutinised by the author's good friend Paul Frampton – a former user doubtless recalling journeys from days-gone-by – whilst the bus was awaiting its next duty on the 75 service to St Luke's Hospital from the Sliema Strand.

At the same time as the Bristol LHs were being acquired a handful of Leyland Tiger Cubs were purchased. Powered by Leyland underfloor engines they were rugged vehicles which lent themselves to rebuilding or rebodying and the Maltese flair and ingenuity was not found wanting. Here DBY 444, a former Blackburn Corporation example has received a major rebuild/new body from Scarnif, producing a very smart looking end result which doubtless should give many years further service to its owner. [JAS both]

The major event of the 'eighties was to be the importation of over 170 Bedfords of various marques, mostly with either Plaxton or Duple coach bodies, in a determined endeavour to upgrade and improve the appearance of the route bus fleet. This took place between 1984 and 1987 – see overleaf.

A few years later three Marshall-bodied units arrived, as seen below with FBY 807 on route 2 to Vittoriosa Town Square, and FBY 708 returning to Sliema Ferry; the other is DBY 467. They had previously been owned by the Atomic Weapons Research Establishment at Aldermaston in Berkshire, and used for staff transport. The bodies were very plain, lacking any embellishment in keeping with their role within the MoD. [DSH, JAS]

A further three Marshall-bodied examples, again on Bedford chassis, arrived around the turn of the decade, having been with Norfolk County Council probably being used for schools' contracts, and similar to examples supplied to the Military. These proved that anything can look smart when given the Maltese treatment, as on Y-0657 (later DBY 657) seen alongside top working the 27 route to Marsaxlokk in 1992. The other two vehicles of this type are registered DBY 495 and FBY 722. [DSH]

The purchase of complete and ready-to-run second-hand vehicles from the UK took a quantum leap forward between 1984 and 1987. Around 170 Plaxton Supreme and Duple Dominant coaches were purchased, based on the Bedford Y-series models with vertical underfloor engines. Some ten Fords of similar layout, also with Plaxton bodies, came at the same time. The effects of this huge influx of almost identical looking vehicles, allowing a similar number of old vehicles to be withdrawn and scrapped, transformed the Malta bus scene and even today there are times when it seems that almost every bus in the Valletta bus station is of one of these types.

This masterly transaction was apparently co-ordinated from Walsingham, in County Durham. Duple and Plaxton's designs were very similar indeed, particularly so in glass sizes and windscreens which were identical and would ease the future spares situation. Both companies were changing their designs at this time, introducing new models and

doubtless looking to clear stocks of trade-in vehicles. Also, history repeating itself perhaps, they and their dealers would have had spares and possibly work in progress they would be glad to dispose of. Did these Bedfords arrive with a dowry of spares inside their saloons and boots, or was there a container load perhaps? If anyone can supply the answers the author would be most interested to hear the full story.

Equally interesting will be the answer as to why for some ten years owners were not allowed to modify the vehicles' large fixed windows which were totally unsuited to Malta's climate, something which must have been obvious even before the purchase was negotiated. Instead, commuters and tourists alike were subjected to the almost unbearable temperatures of Maltese summers. One change which was effected was that many of the bodies were soon fitted with bus seats, but some have retained the high-backed coach seating with which they were originally equipped. [JAS]

In 1995 it was finally agreed, after much lobbying, that the fixed windows of these route buses could be replaced by part-sliders, and this was done as shown on the photographs opposite and on this page. Note that DBY 355 is one of the Ford examples, very much in a minority. Some others of the mass importation which would be used as unscheduled vehicles – coaches – were fitted with air conditioning. Below is an example from an even smaller minority – a Duple Dominant bus. This example had been in service on the Isle of Wight, another had seen service in Norfolk, but they remain rarities. The side advertising panel is for sports wear; others carried here frequently promote bus travel and concessionary ticketing arrangements. [JAS above and right; DSH below]

It might be thought that with the huge numbers of imports − approaching 250 or half the total route bus fleet − the variety and mystique of the Malta bus is becoming a thing of the past. Not so, happily, as this double spread of pictures shows.

Four buses on the facing page hide very different origins or chassis. Top left, DBY 429, originally a Leyland Hippo lorry, has been on the island at least since 1940. It was rebodied by Scarnif in 1995 with elements of Plaxton or Duple front end componentry. [DSH]

FBY 768, upper right, is a Dennis Falcon with bodywork by East Lancashire Coachbuilders and formerly operated in the Hyndburn (Accrington, Lancashire) fleet. [AWD]

EBY 498 is an AEC Reliance dating from 1956, originally registered VWE 258 and carrying a Burlingham Seagull body when it operated for Sheffield United Tours. It then spent some three years with John Laing Construction on staff transport before final withdrawal in the UK. Its stylish new body was built by Aquilina around 1973, almost certainly incorporating Duple front end sections. Note the distinctive glass cantrail lights. [JAS]

DBY 330, lower right, is based on a Ford Cargo lorry chassis. The body, by Ramco, dates from 1999. The unusual windscreen is formed from a pair of Plaxton side windows producing a very distinctive and quite handsome vehicle. [AWD]

DBY 460, seen on this page, is a Brincat-bodied Bedford SB and the front dome design is particularly neat, incorporating a destination box which is actually used! The 652 is one of the 'direct' or express routes, all of which command a premium fare. [PG]

The number of Bedford SB conversions to be found in service reflects two aspects of the model's success, its longevity and output: it was in production from 1950 until 1986 and during that time over 57,000 examples of the chassis were produced. Spare parts will thus have presented little problem for the Maltese bus engineers and converters.

One of the island's best kept secrets is the existence of six open-topped double-deckers – unfortunately for various reasons, including concerns about danger to top-deck passengers from overhanging balconies, none is able to be operated in service and, accordingly, no registration numbers have been allocated. When these pictures were taken the only registration marks carried were the original UK ones on the rear of the buses!

Notwithstanding such rather trifling matters, Hugh Barker captured these views during a carnival-type procession to mark the successful pro-Euro Campaign in April 2003 when Malta's decision to enter into the European Union on MayDay 2004 was celebrated. All three former Thamesdown Daimler Fleetlines were hired by the Maltese Nationalist Party and on the facing page what had been UMR 193T leads a convoy along Sliema seafront, en route to St Julians. It allegedly included some rather dubious and, also, unlicensed old cars – apparently there had been some sort of unofficial legal amnesty for the day! As to insurance, probably better not to ask. Such was the reception that the convoy was brought to a standstill several times.

The island acquired this second generation of open-toppers when five Daimler Fleetlines and one Daimler CVG6 were purchased in 1993, three Fleetlines by Garden of Eden and these three vehicles by Cancu Coaches. All the open top vehicles used in the celebrations belonged to Cancu – perhaps Garden of Eden support the other party? Either way it seems likely that when the implications of joining the EU have been digested – certainly insofar as they will affect the bus owners and drivers – they will not give rise to another such procession.

The rear-engined Fleetlines were all bodied by the erstwhile Eastern Coach Works of Lowestoft. If or when it does become possible to use them they will surely become a major tourist attraction. Cancu's red-liveried UMR 192T is seen, lower right, whilst the other white liveried one (note the mirror-image destination layout) UMR 191T is seen also awaiting the return of its passengers at the Valletta bus park; apparently they were attending a Sunday victory rally whose noise had to be witnessed to be believed.

[HB all three]

Time to change working conditions, practices and the fleet's age profile ?

The Maltese bus engineers are second to none when it comes to making old vehicles work – their workmanship rivals that of many of the best preservationists and yet they are doing this to keep their buses in daily service to earn themselves and their families a living. However, backyard repairs, conversions and partly-mended patch-painted vehicles as shown here may start to become a thing of the past.

In common with many other countries Malta has good reason to be aware of the increasing congestion and pollution which rising numbers of private cars are creating. Accordingly in the mid-nineteen nineties decisions were taken which would address these problems. New standards with a better image for public transport were drawn up, to encourage greater use of the buses by commuters. A newer fleet, with easier access and cleaner engine emissions was seen as essential. Clearly there would be a huge cost implication and events moved very slowly. The owners had many reservations, especially as the plan envisaged reducing the fleet from 508 route buses to c300.

For various reasons, mainly financial, the whole process took much longer than expected, and there were also strings attached to the deal involving the installation of ticket machines on the buses, the introduction of pre-paid magnetic cards for registering and paying for journeys, and changes in working hours and traditional day-on-day-off routines. Discussions concerning these matters are still on-going as we closed for press in February 2004.

Eventually, to move things forward, five sample low-floor 'green engined' buses were ordered from the UK, and these were delivered during 1997 as shown over the next three pages.
[RGR lower right; PG others]

The start of the low-floor revolution was marked by the arrival in spring 1997 of five vehicles built in the UK, and designed to meet the Malta Government's new requirements for easier access, and cleaner exhaust emissions. This view, taken in Marsaxlokk in April 1999, clearly demonstrates the lower step height. Photographed just below the church, this area is now pedestrianised. Note that the prevalence of dropping passengers away from kerbs and pavements makes the low floor entrance even more desirable. Ease of boarding and alighting is self-evident by the relaxed attitude of the passengers. FBY 805 was destined to be the only example of the Optare model from Leeds in Yorkshire. [JAS]

Four Dennis Darts followed shortly after the Optare Excel, seen on the previous page. East Lancashire Coachbuilders of Blackburn, Lancashire, supplied two examples of its Spryte model, as seen facing, which arrived in March 1997, whilst Transbus fielded two examples of the Pointer from the Plaxton Scarborough factory in Yorkshire, as seen above. These arrived in May 1997. Like the Optare Excel these vehicles were all equipped with air suspension offering a very different type of ride from the ruggedly steel-sprung existing fleet.

The potential orders from the island were considerable. The daily requirements for over 250 service buses are supplemented by extras from the unscheduled fleet, or those on days off. World-wide interest was aroused and enquiries – all resulting in orders – were to come from Turkey, China, Poland, Greece and Macedonia.

The big problem was always going to be the cost of these buses. With the very tight margins involved in operation, because the Government is resisting any increases in ticket prices, the cost of these buses is having to be met very largely by the Government. In addition to the Government grant of Lm32,000, ie £53,000, the operators were required to find as a deposit a sum of Lm13,000, equivalent to some £22,000 per vehicle, payable over a period of up to ten years. It should be remembered here that most of those required to make this investment are one-man one-bus operators, and that they will also be required to commit to contract maintenance on the vehicles through the agents, something they would have done themselves on the old buses. Out of 508 buses available for service there are around 400 of these owner-operators. [JAS]

Doubtless the resolution of this thorny financial problem accounted for much of the seven year gestation period, during which the five new UK built vehicles demonstrated their capabilities. Although they have performed quite well their price, as ever, was to be a problem. An attempt to resolve matters by using locally built bodies on suitable imported chassis followed, shown in the next pages, but the eventual solution was to be very different as will be seen shortly.

Meanwhile, DBY 307, facing, and FBY 742 seen on this page were photographed at Sliema ferry terminus, working the 'direct' route 645 between Sliema and Cirkewwa, the two ferry terminals, during April 2000. The upper detail view is of interest since it shows one of the few instances when destination blinds were in use. The yellow on black is clearly to UK Diptac specification but be they black, white or yellow they were short lived and where blinds are used only the route numbers are displayed now. The left hand view gives a foretaste of things to come – gone are the days of attractive curvaceous rears – the styling of all the new buses has a marked affinity to the shape of the high rise properties being built to meet the needs of the growing tourism market as seen in the background.

Note that the bodybuilders were aware of the owners' liking for ornamentation and had given them a head start with a selection of badges being attached before the bus left the factory! [JAS both left; DSH above and below]

The Sliema ferry arriving from Valletta, mentioned also on page 18.

Whilst the cost of imported buses was likely to be a major obstacle, the loss of opportunities for body building on the island must also have weighed heavily on some minds. The next development in the modernisation plan addressed this. Scarnif had already produced some interesting rebodyings on earlier chassis, including a Leyland Tiger Cub which was completed during 2002, and clearly had the ability, the will and the flair to tackle the low floor challenge.

They duly bodied a Volvo B6BLE low floor chassis, completed in March 2002, and, after certification by the Technical Board of the Transport Authority, registered it as FBY 727. Transport Minister Censu Galea presided over the launch on 3rd May of that year. Subsequently a similar body appeared on a MAN 14.200 which appeared as EBY 488. The MAN was evidently favoured, partly because it met Euro3 emission levels which the Government had now decided to adopt as its standard, and at least a further four MANs have been bodied since. These attractive buses fulfil the requirements for easy access and low emissions but the cost and need for volume production were still serious considerations, since as already mentioned some 250 buses would need to be produced and neither Scarnif or any one else on Malta had that volume of production capacity.

Examples of bodies on both types of chassis are seen here, suitably badged, and demonstrating the flair which the designer has incorporated into the front end profile. An interior view of EBY 488, opposite lower left, shows the light and airy interior and the handrails with integral bell pushes and low level strap hangers.

The large eye-catching SCARNIF lettering – an anagram of Francis, the builder – on the front panel of the latest buses is commendable since they stand out in the bus station. Journey times are often such that vehicles soon reappear from some destinations, and also move around within the loading areas to take waiting time off the stand.

The net result in October 2003 was to give the impression that there were many more of these bodies in service than there actually are!

Note the bright red brand-new Almex ticket machine; the separate card reader is hidden in this view. [JAS]

The view above shows the clean lines of the new body design, here on the first MAN, EBY 488, with an interior view of the same bus. Note the handrails, of European style and possibly manufacture. [JAS both]

Scarnif are also responsible for building many of the Malta and Gozo mini coaches, and one is seen here in the distinctive deep red livery which they all carry. This 18 coach-seated example, IMY 400, is a Scarnif-Saftrans production. [PG]

China has become a major player in world manufacturing, and with its economy growing at over 9% in 2003 some analysts now regard it as the world's powerhouse. Not surprisingly, a slice of this output is in bus manufacture and even before the latest spectacular growth the Chinese revolution in Malta was marked by the arrival in 2001 of this King Long built coach, registered LCY 907, purchased and operated by SMS Tours of Zejtun, trading as Cancu Supreme. Proprietor Nazzareno Abela also owns the Optare Excel seen in Marsaxlokk on page 65, and is the Agent on Malta for Globus Bus & Coach Industries of Birmingham, the distributors of the Macedonian MCII buses from Skopje, one of which is seen on page 79.

China had been represented on the island in the dockyard, of course, but this was the first foray into the realms of land transport. It was to be a significant purchase in the evolution of the new fleet of Maltese public transport, being followed in 2003 by a large batch of integral buses from the same source which are scattered around the island's bus operators.

The now-familiar King Long chrome emblem can be seen on the front panel whilst the large 'praying mantis' type driver's mirrors would soon become a familiar sight on the buses, albeit with white backs rather than black as seen here. [AWD]

A further Chinese vehicle, this time a dual-door bus, arrived in April 2002, and clearly displayed its origins. The Chongqing Auto Factory is owned by the China Urban Bus and Construction Corporation which has a number of factories in China. It was photographed in spring 2002. As far as is known it has not yet entered service in Malta and it would seem unlikely that it ever will, or at least in this form. Apart from the dual-door configuration the vehicle has a high floor and the leg room for many of the seats is somewhat cramped by European standards, particularly above the wheelarches. It does, however, have a wheelchair lift at the centre door which could conceivably result in a use being found for it. Kia Motors of Qormi are handling both King Long and Chongqing vehicles on the island.

Whatever the problems in securing approval for such vehicles to operate, they are only part of the wider situation of changing the whole ethos of bus operation in Malta. Those who have laboured long and hard to find the right machines at the right price and to import them from far and wide may now find tough battles ahead before all the old buses and routines are replaced. [JAS]

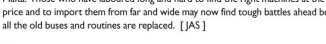

Modernisation – at what price?

The Maltese Government's decision to upgrade its public transport system is both brave and far-reaching in its aims. Whether all its aspirations can be achieved – certainly in the short timescale – remains to be seen.

Fundamental to its policy is the need to address the alarming fall in numbers of commuters using the buses; whether this vicious circle is entirely due to the ever-increasing number of cars on the island, or the state of the buses, or a combination of both, is open to discussion. It is claimed that the drop in passenger numbers has consistently been around one million per year from 1996 to date, and the increasing congestion on the roads, together with the associated deterioration of air quality, all highlight the need for change.

The intention to seek membership of the European Union, taken way back in the 'nineties, brought these, and other, matters to the forefront. If membership was going to require a steady upgrading of many facilities, including transport, better to grasp the nettle sooner rather than later seemed both logical and praiseworthy. A good example is the decision to set Euro3 as the emission level for engines, and also to require new buses to be low floor and to have access for the disabled. Improved roads, better bus shelters, more versatile ticketing arrangements and automatic vehicle locating systems to aid timekeeping and reliability are also part of the package.

Clearly, the downside to such worthy aspirations is the cost, and the Government has had to make provision, through the Bank of Valletta, to assist in the purchase of the new technologically advanced buses. The Transport Authority then launched, as part of the modernisation plan, the new ticketing arrangements, revised working schedules for drivers, and, most contentious of all, confirmed its intention to reduce the number of bus licences from 508 to c300.

It can be imagined that whatever views the owner drivers might have on ticketing and schedule changes would be as nought compared to the reduction of 40% in the fleet size. The matter of driver's hours will also be a not insignificant matter. As this book closed for press the influx of new vehicles was clear for all to see. What was less clear, bubbling below the surface but reported daily in the *Malta Times* and *Independent* newspapers is the unrest which is taking place, manifesting itself in many unexpected ways in addition to the predictable periodic strike action.

It will be interesting to see in the months ahead just how the two entrenched positions can be reconciled. Meanwhile, whatever happens, some aspects of the bus scene are going to change out of all recognition. We wish both sides well in the resolution of the thorny problems they are going to have to address and resolve.

The shape of the future – the two main contenders for the new bus market appear to be the Chinese King Long and the Turkish BMC Maltese Falcon, seen here in Valletta's bus station in November 2003. At that time there were 35 King Longs and 29 Falcons in service, with more on order or waiting to go into service. [JAS]

Waiting to return from Birkirkara, October 2003. The engine is switched off and the electronic destination display ceases to function. [JAS]

At the time of writing the most numerous of the new generation low-floor buses were the Chinese King Longs, the products of a manufacturing company founded in 1988, owned by a consortium of Chinese companies. Reference has already been made to the part which manufacturing is playing in the Chinese economy. It may be interesting to note that there are 160 bus manufacturers in the country, of which King Long is of major significance, if not the major player.

Designated XMQ6113GMC, it is integral in construction, and fitted with a Cummins 260 Euro3 engine built in Darlington, England. Seating 45 passengers, with air conditioning as an option, they are reputedly the most competitively priced of the various imports. Electronic displays show temperature, time and destination number but, unhelpfully, the destination display goes off when the engine is switched off at the terminus. The first King Long bus appeared in July 2001, registered FBY 782, and there was a ceremony to welcome the vehicle before it entered service.

DBY 443, seen opposite at Birkirkara, shows the clean lines of the design; it replaced a Dodge, as did DBY 430, seen above with Chinese lettering across the front, in the bus station.

A rear view of EBY 510 shows yet another square cut design, with prominent cooling louvres for the engine compartment.

The invitation to visit the dealers, left, is one of the few documents we have found which is actually printed throughout in Maltese. [PG top and left; JAS top right]

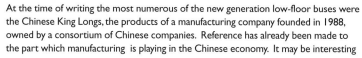

FALCON
1100
CITY BUS

BMC

Information on most of the new-generation buses is far from easy to find. The exception is the Turkish BMC Maltese Falcon whose origins can be found with Marshalls of Cambridge. Produced very much to meet the Maltese bus operator's requirements, but also to comply with UK regulations, the vehicle has a separate chassis, and of traditional 'U' section rather than the box-section so much favoured in recent years. It is built from heavier than normal gauge steel for added strength to cope with the infamous road surfaces.

Similarly the stainless steel framed body is also constructed from thicker gauge metal, and for the same reasons. All this adds up to a seriously heavyweight vehicle with an all-up GVW of 17 tonnes.

A full specification of the vehicle has been released, printed on the reverse of the attractive promotional flyer illustrated alongside. Salient features include overall length of 11-metres, (the maximum permissible in Malta); overall width 2.5 metres; seating for 45 (the statutory requirement for all the new generation buses); Cummins 220 ISBe Euro3 engine (manufactured in Darlington); Voith 4-speed automatic transmission with integral retarder; maximum road speed of 100kph (though not on Maltese roads where the maximum permitted limit on country roads is 40 mph – but only 24 mph in built up areas); wheelchair accessibility; optional air conditioning; and, considered to be extremely important, full-size – 8.25 x 25.5 – wheels.

As with the other new generation vehicles servicing and warranty arrangements are an essential part of the purchase contract and International Auto Centre of Qormi are handling this aspect of the vehicle's lives in Malta.

As mentioned, the vehicle has also been designed with the UK market in mind, and one was displayed at Coach and Bus, NEC Birmingham, in September 2003, where it attracted considerable interest. Orders were subsequently confirmed from the former English municipalities of Chester and Warrington, as well as two or three Welsh independents. In a twist of fate it was announced in January 2004 that 100 Maltese drivers have been recruited to drive for two other Welsh independents from May 1st 2004, the date from which movement within the EU allows Maltese workers to come to the UK. It would be ironic if these drivers found themselves driving Maltese Falcons in Wales in years to come.

By November 2003 some 40 examples had been delivered to their new owners on Malta and the Agent, Charles Micallef, was confident of supplying many more. He had committed to a production run of 100 machines from the Izmir factory over a period of twelve months. The vehicle's Cummins engine and Voith gearbox with integral retarder gives a powerful and impressive ride with smooth performance. The BMC organisation in Turkey has a factory which build Cummins engines under licence, but only to Euro2 level. It is for this reason that the vehicles are fitted with Darlington-built power units. Readers of this book unable to visit Malta can thus sample the vehicles nearer home and the UK trade press is following their progress.

Only one of the Falcons carries the Marshall badge – perhaps there are copyright issues to be resolved – and it is seen here proudly displaying it. The badge was affixed by no less a person than Clive McNally, the Proprietor and Chairman of BMC. The clean lines, particularly the frontal aspect, are well portrayed in this view. [HB]

Charles Micallef told the Author, after a demonstration run in FBY 753 in October 2003, that distribution of the BMCs through his organisation in Malta would be a well-set-up operation, and that in addition to sales, maintenance and repairs would be carried out. A couple of days later the message was reinforced by this sign in a shop window in Mdina, the Silent City. Though the lady was temporarily out of stock she was confident that supplies would soon be available again; perhaps we were not talking about the same product ! [JAS]

The first of the Volvo Saracakis buses to reach Malta is seen here outside the Volvo agent's premises in Luqa, having just arrived from the Customs Compound at Valletta docks, still bearing its Greek registration plates and carrying a red trial-run plate in the windscreen, presumably an equivalent of a British trade plate. It had been driven overland in Greece to Italy by the Agent and the saloon was packed with spares including a replacement windscreen and spare seats along with a sprig of lucky heather in the sliding window to the right of the driver. The first of five delivered by November 2003, this bus became FBY 741. [HB]

The body designer's approach to the rear engine layout varies from maker to maker. This is perhaps not the neatest external shape of the new generation vehicles, but the interior is neat and the colour scheme is pleasing. The discreet badging on the rear panel confirms the vehicle's identity as a Volvo B7R.

FBY 758, seen in the bus station before the road improvements of late 2003 were completed, replaced a Bedford conversion from a chassis which had previously been an MoD crane. These are the pearls which future enthusiasts will miss – an entry recording the demise of a Volvo B7R will not have quite the same charisma when it is withdrawn in years to come !

Note the rear destination blinds, not in use of course. There is a distinct air of *deja-vu* in some of these situations – we could almost be back in the bad old UK days of the late '70s early '80s where unused destination blinds are concerned. Whether the electronic indicators will also be consigned to oblivion remains to be seen. [JAS]

Badging has always been a part of the scene and the new imports have introduced yet more variety. This is the front of what became FBY 741, and, as can be clearly seen, with the Greek bodybuilder's badge above the Volvo logo with its diagonal bar. Note also the wheelchair logo on the nearside corner; all the new generation vehicles must have doorways wide enough to accept wheelchairs and a place for the chair to be parked safely inside the bus alongside a seat for a carer or companion. By November 2003 there were five Saracakis bodies to be seen – DBY 454, EBY 598, FBY 741, FBY 745 and FBY 758. [HB]

Further imports into the new fleet came in 2002 with the arrival of three Polish built Solaris integrally-built Urbino buses, the first of which was approved by the Maltese Transport Authority in August of that year. Built in the Poznan factory of Solaris Bus & Coach, which produces both buses and trolleybuses, they incorporate the manufacturer's immediately recognisable neat front end design, together with a very clean-and-tidy interior layout and finish.

The vehicle is basically the manufacturer's European standard low floor bus, with relatively minor modifications for use in Malta. Powered by the Iveco NEF F4AE0681B engine to Euro3 emission level standards, with the DAF PF 183C as an alternative option, Malta's examples are equipped with Voith gearboxes and transmission. One of the Solaris owner/drivers reported that the fuel consumption is high and that he would prefer a manual box to improve the mpg. The question of consumption is a delicate one – an enquiry as to hard figures often elicits the respose "oh, about Lm16 per day " – the local equivalent of the length of a piece of string perhaps ! The 45-seater integral vehicle is 10.9 metres long and this model has been named the Solaris Valetta, but note the spelling.

As with all the imports, an agency and distributorship has been arranged on the island, and Exalco Holdings Ltd based in St George's Bay will be looking after matters.

FBY 752, seen above at Golden Bay in October 2003, replaced the former Diamond T carrying that number. Note the new bus shelter being built in the background. [PG]

Another source of imports has come from MCII (Motor Coach Industries International) whose factory is in Skopje, Macedonia, a company probably better known to bus enthusiasts from its American parent, Motor Coach Industries. In November 2003, three of these MAN-engined vehicles, at least one of which had a manual gearbox, were in service, registered DBY 440, EBY 621 and FBY 760. The first two of these registrations had not been in use since around 1998; FBY 760 had been carried by an International with a Sammut 36-seat body. The original order had apparently been for eight such vehicles, but this was reduced because of late delivery.

The first of the trio, DBY 440, is seen here on an initial test run before entering revenue service at St Georges Bay in April 2003, where it demonstrated a fair turn of speed, much to the chagrin of the photographer. [HB]

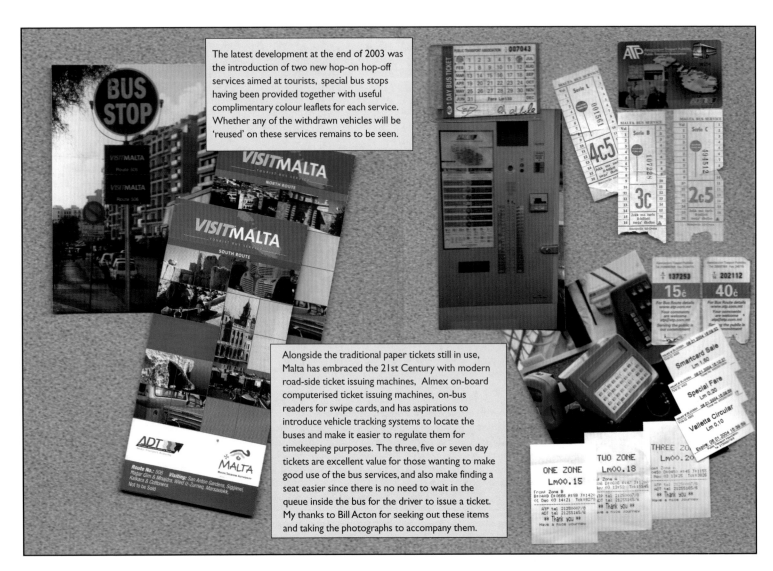

The latest development at the end of 2003 was the introduction of two new hop-on hop-off services aimed at tourists, special bus stops having been provided together with useful complimentary colour leaflets for each service. Whether any of the withdrawn vehicles will be 'reused' on these services remains to be seen.

Alongside the traditional paper tickets still in use, Malta has embraced the 21st Century with modern road-side ticket issuing machines, Almex on-board computerised ticket issuing machines, on-bus readers for swipe cards, and has aspirations to introduce vehicle tracking systems to locate the buses and make it easier to regulate them for timekeeping purposes. The three, five or seven day tickets are excellent value for those wanting to make good use of the bus services, and also make finding a seat easier since there is no need to wait in the queue inside the bus for the driver to issue a ticket. My thanks to Bill Acton for seeking out these items and taking the photographs to accompany them.

Acknowledgements, Bibliography and Photographic attributes.

I would like to thank all those people who have given their time to assist in this publication. There has been a genuine desire to cover the Maltese bus scene in a manner which would satisfy those who have seen the buses at first hand whilst also encouraging those who have not yet made the pilgrimage to do so. Accordingly, I express my sincere thanks to :– Bill Acton; John Banks; Hugh Barker; Alan Drabble; Peter Gascoine; Scott Hellewell; Revd. Eric Ogden; Bob Rowe; John Seale; David and Mary Shaw; Bob Smith; Ian Stubbs; Peter Trevaskis; Paul Wigan; and, last but by no means least, my son Mark for partly-taming the recalcitrant computers.

Photographs have come from the author's camera [JAS] and also those of Bill Acton [BA]; Hugh Barker [HB]; Alan Drabble [AWD]; Peter Gascoine [PG]; Scott Hellewell [DSH]; Josie Rowe – with Bob on the shutter – [RGR]; Ian Stubbs [IS]; Peter Trevaskis [PT] and Paul Wigan [PW].

Research has been carried out on the island over a period of years under the pretext of holidays in the sunshine, but more recently information on the new vehicles has been culled from the British trade and enthusiast journals, notably *Bus and Coach Buyer*; *Coach and Bus Week*; *Classic Bus*; and *Buses*. *Malta – The Bus Kingdom* helped find a different perspective. The PSV Circle lists have provided details of the vehicles and their histories, as also has *The Malta Bus Handbook*. *The Malta Buses*, by Bonnici and Cassar was both fascinating and invaluable. The *Malta Times* and *Independent* newspapers were also very useful as were their web sites. Hugh Barker and Bob Rowe have also found reams of material from various other web sites from the island. The Transport Authority's various leaflets and other official publications have filled in much detail. Air Malta's house magazine has been useful, as have many of the guide books available in the shops.

I am grateful to those included in the above who have read the proofs and made valuable suggestions but at the end of the day any errors they have missed are still down to me.

John A. Senior.   Glossop, Derbyshire, England.   February 2004.

Gone but not forgotten . . . .

"a bit of TLC and this one could be a runner" the advert said . . .

"did you remember to bring the jump leads Marco?"